JEFF GORDON

DISCOVER THE LIFE OF A SPORTS STAR

David and Patricia Armentrout

Rourke
Publishing LLC
Vero Beach, Florida 32964

www.rourkepublishing.com

PHOTO CREDITS: All photos © Getty Images

Title page: *Jeff's car leads the pack at the Pepsi 400 in 1999.*

Editor: Frank Sloan

Cover and interior design by Nicola Stratford

Library of Congress Cataloging-in-Publication Data

Armentrout, David, 1962-
  Jeff Gordon / David Armentrout and Patricia Armentrout.
    v. cm. — (Discover the life of a sports star)
Includes bibliographical references (p.) and index.
Contents: Meet Jeff Gordon — Passion for racing — A future in stock car racing — Rookie of the year — The Winston Cup Series — Number 24 — That winning feeling — Highs and lows — The championship.
  ISBN 1-58952-653-8 (hardcover)
  1. Gordon, Jeff, 1971—Juvenile literature. 2. Automobile racing drivers—United States—Biography—Juvenile literature. [1. Gordon, Jeff, 1971- 2. Automobile racing drivers.] I. Armentrout, Patricia, 1960- II. Title. III. Series: Armentrout, David, 1962-   Discover the life of a sports star.
  GV1032.G67A76 2003
  796.72'092—dc21

                                                    2003005933

Printed in the USA

CG/CG

Table of Contents

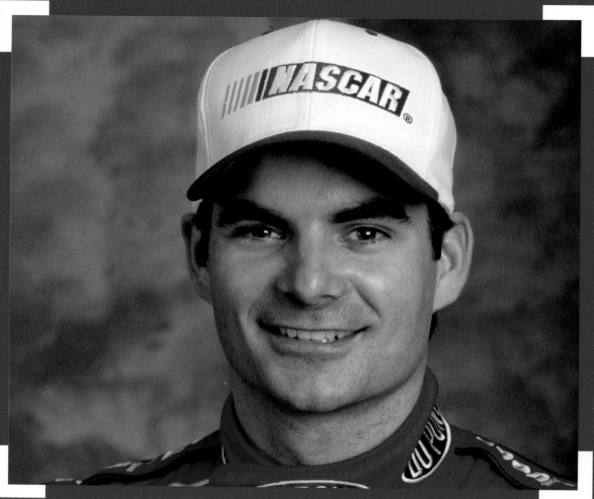

Jeff Gordon is one of the most popular stock car drivers in NASCAR's history.

Meet Jeff Gordon

Jeff Gordon is a stock car driver. He experienced the thrill of racing at a very early age. Today, Jeff's life is fueled by the fast-paced sport of automobile racing.

Born: August 4, 1971 in Vallejo, California
Competition: NASCAR's Winston and Busch Series
Car: Chevrolet Monte Carlo
Number: 24
Record: Winston Cup Champ in 1995, 97, 98, and 2001

Passion for Racing

Jeff's passion for racing began at the age of four. He competed in bicycle motocross (BMX) events. Jeff then moved on to racing quarter midgets and go-karts. Quarter midgets are small cars that sit low to the ground. Go-karts are small, too, but they have more powerful engines than quarter midgets do. Jeff also raced midget cars and sprint cars. Sprint cars are full-sized automobiles with very powerful engines.

Sprint cars have roll bars to protect drivers from injuries.

Jeff learned about driving stock cars at the Buck Baker driving school in North Carolina.

A Future in Stock Car Racing

Jeff and his family traveled all over the country so Jeff could race. Success came naturally for Jeff. By 1991 he had more than 500 wins under his belt. Jeff decided it was time to commit to one type of car. He went to North Carolina to a stock car racing school. It didn't take long for Jeff to decide that stock car racing was his future.

NASCAR's Winston Cup Series draws more than six million spectators each season.

Rookie of the Year

Jeff raced his first full season in the Busch Grand National **Series** in 1991. His past racing experience and his standings at the end of the season won Jeff **Rookie** of the Year.

The Busch series is the second highest level of competition in **NASCAR**. It is considered to be a training ground for the Winston Cup Series.

*Jeff celebrates a Winston Cup
win with car owner Rick Hendrick (far right).*

The Winston Cup Series

Near the end of the 1992 racing season Rick Hendrick signed Jeff on to his Winston Cup racing team. Hendrick runs a company that designs, builds, and races stock cars.

Jeff began the 1993 season with a list of goals. One goal was finishing his first Winston Cup season as Rookie of the Year, and he did.

Number 24

Jeff's car was unveiled at the North Carolina Motor Speedway in 1993. The colorful Chevrolet Monte Carlo, with the number 24, impressed everyone.

Like other stock cars, Jeff's car is a modified version of a passenger car. It's driven on paved oval tracks at speeds that can exceed 200 miles (320 kilometers) an hour. Jeff's **pit crew** is called the Rainbow Warriors, after the colors of his car.

A pit crew has only 20 seconds to refuel, change tires, and make minor adjustments.

That Winning Feeling

Jeff won his first Winston Cup race at the Charlotte Motor Speedway in 1994. The race was the Coca-Cola 600, the longest NASCAR race in the series. That same year Jeff won the first Brickyard 400. It took place at the Indianapolis Motor Speedway, the same track where the famous Indy 500 race runs. Indy 500 drivers race Formula One-type cars, not stock cars.

Jeff receives a kiss after winning the Brickyard 400 in 1994.

Earnhardt's number 3 car is right behind Gordon's number 24 in the 1999 Daytona 500.

Highs and Lows

Jeff began the 1997 season winning the Daytona 500. At 25, Jeff was the youngest driver ever to win that race. Jeff won the Daytona 500 again in 1999. It was one of his best career races. Jeff's superior driving held off racing legend Dale Earnhardt for the win.

Unfortunately, the rest of the 1999 season had its share of lows. Jeff had car trouble and was not able to complete seven of his races. He finished the season in 6th place, which was an "off" year for Jeff.

The Championship

Drivers are awarded points in a NASCAR race. Winners earn 175 points. Points decline for drivers who come in second, third, and so on. However, drivers can earn bonus points in several categories. For example, five bonus points are earned for leading a **lap**.

The driver with the most points at the end of a season wins the Championship Cup. Jeff Gordon won the Winston Cup Championship in 1995, 1997, 1998, and again in 2001. He ended the 2005 season with four wins, and became the fifth driver to win three Daytona 500s.

Jeff celebrates his 2001 Winston Cup Championship.

Dates to Remember

1971 Born in Vallejo, California, August 4

1991 Wins Rookie of the Year for the Busch
    Grand National Series

1993 Wins Rookie of the Year for the Winston
    Cup Series

1994 Wins first Winston Cup race

1995 Wins the Winston Cup Championship

1997 Wins the Daytona 500 and the Winston
    Cup Championship

1998 Wins the Winston Cup Championship

1999 Wins the Daytona 500, beating legendary
    Dale Earnhardt

2001 Wins the Winston Cup Championship

2005 Wins Daytona 500

Glossary

lap (LAP) — a single time around a track

NASCAR — National Association for Stock Car Auto Racing: the governing body for the Winston Cup, Craftsman Truck, and Busch Grand National series, among others

pit crew (PIT KROO) — a team of people who change tires, refuel, and make repairs or other adjustments during a race

rookie (ROOK ee) — a first-year driver

series (SIHR eez) — a group of races that make up one season

Index

Further Reading

Benson, Michael. *Jeff Gordon: NASCAR Driver*. Ferguson Publications, 2005.
Leebrick, Kristal. *Jeff Gordon*. Capstone Press, 2004.
Gigliotti, Jim. *Jeff Gordon: Simply the Best*. Tradition Books, 2003.

Websites To Visit

www.jeffgordon.com
www.nascar.com
www.gordonline.com

About The Authors

David and Patricia Armentrout have written many nonfiction books for young readers. They have had several books published for primary school reading. The Armentrouts live in Cincinnati, Ohio, with their two children.